While You're Still You

A Guided Journal for Early-Stage Dementia Caregivers

The In-Between
Book 2

L J Ribar

The In-Between Series
Honest Books for Life's Hardest Seasons

Some of the hardest seasons in life live in the space between diagnosis and whatever comes next. The In-Between is a series of short, honest books for people in that space — caregivers, spouses, adult children, and anyone loving someone through a passage that frightens them both. Each book is written for a specific journey. All of them are written for you.

* * *

Sharing the Long Goodbye
A Companion for Families Facing Terminal Illness

While You're Still You
A Guided Journal for Early-Stage Dementia Caregivers

Still Your Child, Still My Parent
A Guided Companion for Caring for Aging Parents

Things Too Heavy to Carry Silently
A Companion Journal for The In-Between series

While You're Still You

A Guided Journal for
Early-Stage Dementia Caregivers

L J Ribar

A Note Before We Begin

You're holding this book because someone you love has received a diagnosis that changes everything—and nothing, yet.

Maybe the word dementia was spoken out loud for the first time in a doctor's office. Maybe you've known something was shifting for months, and the diagnosis only confirmed what your gut already understood. Either way, you're standing at the beginning of something you didn't choose, and nobody handed you a map.

This is not a medical textbook. It won't give you a treatment plan or walk you through the neuroscience of what's happening in your loved one's brain. Other books do that, and some of them are very good. This one is different.

This is a companion for the in-between. For the season when your person is still very much here—still laughing at old jokes, still humming songs from decades ago, still reaching for your hand—but something is quietly, unmistakably changing. A season when the rest of the world may not see what you see. When you're expected to carry on as normal while privately learning to hold two truths at once: they're still here, and they're slowly leaving.

There is no right way to feel. Grief, relief, fear, frustration, fierce love—they can all live in the same hour. They often do.

Inside these pages you'll find three things:

Understanding. What's happening, what to expect, and why this stage is harder than most people realize.

Practical tools. Simple ways to track patterns, prepare for appointments, and build the support you'll need.

Space to remember. Prompted pages for preserving stories, capturing moments, and doing the sacred work of remembering together—while you still can.

* * *

How to Use This Book

However you need to. There's no correct order. You don't have to start at the beginning or finish by a certain date. Some sections will matter to you right now; others might not be relevant for months. Some pages are for reading. Some are for writing. Some are for sitting with on a hard day, just to feel less alone.

Skip what doesn't serve you. Return to what does. Write in the margins. Dog-ear the pages. This book is meant to be used, not preserved.

You're doing something that requires more courage, patience, and love than most people will ever understand. You won't do it perfectly. Nobody does. But you're here, and that matters more than you know.

Let's begin.

Part One
Understanding the Terrain

Chapter 1
What Early-Stage Actually Looks Like

arly-stage dementia is a land of contradictions.

Your person might tell a vivid, detailed story from 1987 and then forget that lunch happened two hours ago. They might navigate a familiar drive perfectly on Tuesday and get turned around on Thursday. They might manage a complicated recipe from memory one evening and stare blankly at the coffeemaker the next morning, unsure what to do with it.

This is the nature of the early stage: it's inconsistent. The losses are real but unpredictable. They appear and retreat. Good days make you wonder if the diagnosis was wrong. Hard days remind you it wasn't.

If you're finding this confusing, that's because it is. And if you're finding it lonely, you're not imagining that either.

The early stage of dementia is often the loneliest—not because no one is around, but because no one else can see what you see.

Friends and family may say things like "They seem fine to me!" or "We all forget things." They're not trying to dismiss you. They simply don't have the vantage point you do. You live in the details— the repeated questions, the misplaced bills, the flicker of confusion that crosses your loved one's face before they cover it with a smile. You see the effort behind what used to be effortless.

That private knowledge can feel like carrying a secret. It helps to name it: you are witnessing something real, even when others can't.

Normal Aging vs. Something More

Everyone forgets things. That's worth saying up front, because the line between normal aging and early dementia can feel blurry—especially when you're watching someone you love and looking for signs.

Here are some general differences. These are not diagnostic criteria, just patterns that clinicians commonly observe:

Normal aging: Occasionally forgetting where you put your keys. **Early dementia:** Forgetting what keys are for.

Normal aging: Sometimes struggling to find the right word. **Early dementia:** Frequently losing track of a conversation or substituting unrelated words.

Normal aging: Forgetting the name of a casual acquaintance. **Early dementia:** Forgetting a close friend's name, or not recognizing a familiar face in an unfamiliar setting.

Normal aging: Misplacing things occasionally and retracing steps to find them. **Early dementia:** Putting things in unusual places and being unable to retrace steps.

The key distinction isn't whether someone forgets—it's whether the forgetting disrupts daily life, and whether it's getting progressively worse. If you're reading this book, chances are you already know the answer.

Why This Stage Matters

There's a reason this book focuses on the early stage, and it's not just because it's the beginning.

This is the window when your loved one can still participate in their own story. They can still tell you about their childhood, their first love, the job that shaped them. They can still choose what matters to them. They can still help you understand who they are—not just who they were, but who they are right now, in this season.

That window is a gift. It's also finite. And while it's open, there are things you can do together that become much harder later.

This book is designed to help you make the most of that window—not by pretending everything is fine, but by being intentional about what you do with the time you have.

Chapter 2
What Changes to Expect

Every person's experience with dementia is different. The type of dementia, the individual's personality, their overall health, their support system—all of these shape the path. There is no single trajectory, no guaranteed timeline, no universal sequence of events.

That said, there are patterns. Knowing what's common can help you recognize what's happening, respond with less panic, and plan with more clarity. Think of what follows as a map of possible terrain —not a predetermined route.

* * *

Memory

This is usually what people notice first, and it's the change most associated with dementia in the public imagination. In the early stage, short-term memory is typically affected more than long-term memory. Your person may vividly recall their wedding day but not remember a conversation from this morning. They may ask the same question several times in an hour without realizing they've already asked it.

You'll also notice what clinicians call "confabulation"—the brain filling in gaps with plausible details that didn't actually happen. This isn't lying. It's the mind doing its best to construct a coherent story from incomplete information. Understanding this can save you a lot of frustration.

Language

Word-finding becomes harder. Your person may pause mid-sentence, searching for a word that used to come easily. They might substitute a related word ("the sitting thing" for "chair") or trail off and lose the thread of what they were saying. Conversations may become shorter or more repetitive.

This can be one of the most heartbreaking changes to witness, especially if your loved one was always articulate. Be patient. Don't finish their sentences unless they ask you to. Give them time. The words are often still in there—they just take longer to find.

Mood and Personality

The person you love may become more anxious, more withdrawn, or more easily frustrated—especially in situations that used to feel manageable. Social gatherings might overwhelm them. Changes in routine can cause distress that seems disproportionate to the situation.

Some people become quieter. Others become more emotional—quicker to cry, quicker to anger, quicker to laugh. Some develop a sweetness or openness that wasn't there before, as the filters that governed their social behavior begin to soften.

These shifts aren't choices. They're the result of changes in the brain. That doesn't make them easier to live with, but it can help to remember that your person isn't doing this on purpose.

. . .

Daily Tasks

Activities that involve multiple steps—cooking a recipe, managing finances, following driving directions—may become harder. Your person might leave tasks half-finished, not because they lost interest but because they lost the sequence. They may need more time with familiar routines and gentle help with unfamiliar ones.

The instinct for many caregivers is to take over completely. Resist it if you can. In the early stage, your loved one can still do many things—they may just need a quieter environment, a simplified process, or a patient prompt to get started. Preserving their independence as long as possible isn't just practical; it's dignifying.

Time and Orientation

Days may start to blur together. Your person might lose track of what day it is, confuse morning and afternoon, or struggle to estimate how much time has passed. They may mix up the order of recent events or place old memories in the wrong decade.

Clocks and calendars can help, but don't be surprised if they aren't enough. Time becomes less reliable as a framework, and your person may lean more on environmental cues—the light outside, the smell of dinner, your presence—to orient themselves.

Not every change will happen. Not every change will happen in this order. This is a landscape, not a checklist. Use it to recognize, not to predict.

What I've Already Noticed
Pause & Reflect

You don't need to have all the answers. You don't even need full sentences. Just write what's true right now.

The first moment I sensed something was changing .

* * *

What others see vs. what I see at home . . .

The hardest part so far has been . . .

* * *

What surprises me most is . . .

Something I want to remember about how they are right now . . .

Part Two

Being Present Now

Chapter 3
Connection Over Correction

There will come a moment—maybe it's already happened—when your loved one says something that isn't true. Not a lie. Not an exaggeration. Just a memory that's shifted, a detail that's drifted, a story that's rearranged itself in the retelling.

Maybe they say they talked to their mother this morning—and their mother has been gone for twenty years. Maybe they tell you about a trip they took last week that actually happened in 1994. Maybe they introduce you to a friend as their sister.

In that moment, you have a choice. And the choice you make will shape the quality of your connection more than almost anything else.

You can be right, or you can be close. In this season, you will rarely get to be both.

The instinct to correct is powerful. It comes from love—from wanting to keep them tethered to reality, from fearing what it means if you don't. But correction, even gentle correction, often causes confusion, shame, and distress. Your person may not remember the facts, but they will feel the emotional residue of being told they're wrong. That feeling can linger long after the conversation fades.

. . .

Entering Their World

What works better, almost every time, is entering their world instead of dragging them back into yours.

When she asks about her mother—gone thirty years now—you might say, "What are you thinking about your mom today?" and let her visit somewhere that feels safe. You're not lying. You're accompanying. You're meeting her where she actually is, not where you wish she were.

Clinicians sometimes call this "therapeutic fibbing," but that term can feel uncomfortable. Think of it instead as emotional honesty. The facts may be wrong, but the feelings are real. Your job isn't to police the facts. It's to honor the feelings.

This doesn't mean you never redirect. If your person is distressed—believing something frightening that isn't true, for example—gentle reassurance and redirection are appropriate. But the goal is comfort, not accuracy.

When They Repeat Themselves

Your person may tell you the same story three times in an hour. They may ask the same question before you've finished answering it. This is one of the most common experiences of early-stage caregiving, and one of the most quietly exhausting.

It helps to remember that for them, it's the first time. Every time. The story feels just as vivid, the question just as urgent, the punchline just as fresh. Your patience in hearing it again is a gift they don't know they're receiving.

When you feel your patience wearing thin—and it will—try shifting your attention from the content to the connection. It doesn't matter that you've heard the story. What matters is that they're reaching for you. Answer that reach.

Tone Over Words

As language becomes harder for your loved one, they'll increasingly rely on tone, facial expression, and body language to understand what's happening around them. They may not follow every word you say, but they will absolutely register how you say it.

A calm voice, a warm expression, a relaxed posture—these communicate safety even when the words don't fully land. Conversely, a sharp tone or frustrated sigh can cause distress that your person can't name but deeply feels.

This isn't about being perfect. You'll lose your patience. You'll snap. You'll feel guilty about it afterward. That's the human part of caregiving. But when you can, lead with warmth. It reaches further than you think.

Chapter 4
Making Memories Now

This might seem like a strange chapter to find in a book about memory loss. But here's what most people don't realize about the early stage: your loved one can still make new memories. They may not hold them as long or as reliably, but the experience of joy, connection, and meaning is real in the moment it happens. And that's enough.

More importantly, this is your window to create the memories that you will carry. The stories you'll tell yourself later, when things are harder. The moments that will remind you who you both were in this season.

You are not just losing memories together. You are still making them. Both things are true.

What Reaches Them

Not everything fades at the same rate. Some channels of connection remain remarkably strong well into dementia. Knowing which ones can help you build moments of genuine closeness, even on difficult days.

Music is often the last thing to go. Songs from your loved one's teens and twenties can light up parts of the brain that seem otherwise unreachable. Play their music. Sing with them. Watch what happens when a familiar melody fills the room—you may see a version of your person you thought was gone.

Smell and taste are powerfully linked to memory. The scent of their mother's perfume, the taste of a childhood dish, fresh coffee, cut grass—these sensory anchors can unlock emotions and associations that words can't reach.

Touch remains meaningful long after verbal communication becomes difficult. Holding hands, brushing hair, sitting close—physical presence communicates love without requiring a single word.

Nature and movement can be deeply calming. A walk in a garden, watching birds, feeling sunlight—the natural world doesn't require memory to be experienced. It just asks you to be present.

Simple Activities That Create Connection

You don't need elaborate plans. Some of the most meaningful moments happen in ordinary settings with ordinary things:

- Play music from their young adult years and let the room fill with it.
- Cook a childhood recipe together, even if they can only help with simple steps.
- Look through old photo albums and let them narrate what they remember.
- Drive past places that mattered to them—the old house, the school, the church.
- Record them telling their favorite stories. Your phone is enough.
- Sit together outside without an agenda.
- Watch a favorite old movie or show—something they know by heart.

- Bring them flowers and ask which ones they like best.

The goal isn't to create a Pinterest-worthy experience. It's to be together in a way that feels good to both of you. Follow their energy. If they're engaged, keep going. If they're tired, stop. The best moments are usually the unhurried ones.

Chapter 5
Communication That Works

As dementia progresses, the way you communicate will need to change. Not because your loved one has become a different person, but because the pathways they use to process language are shifting. What worked before—complex sentences, open-ended questions, rapid conversation—may now create confusion or frustration.

This isn't about talking down to them. It's about removing obstacles so the real connection can get through.

Slow Down

This is the single most important change you can make. Speak a little more slowly. Leave pauses. Give them time to process what you've said before you say the next thing. Silence isn't failure—it's space.

Many caregivers unconsciously speed up when they're anxious or impatient. Notice when it happens. Take a breath. The conversation will go better for both of you.

. . .

Simplify, Don't Patronize

Use shorter sentences. Offer one idea at a time. But keep your tone adult and respectful. There's a vast difference between simplifying your language and talking to someone like a child. Your loved one may struggle with processing, but they are not a child. Speak to who they still are.

Choose Over Open-Ended

"What do you want for dinner?" is a surprisingly hard question when your brain is struggling with executive function. The options are infinite and the retrieval process is exhausting.

"Would you like soup or a sandwich?" is much easier. Two concrete options. A simple choice. Autonomy without overwhelm.

Apply this principle broadly: Would you like to walk in the park or sit in the garden? The blue shirt or the green one? This movie or that one? Choices preserve dignity. Open-ended questions, however well-intentioned, can create anxiety.

Use Their Name

Before you start a conversation, say their name. Make eye contact. Make sure you have their attention before you begin. This simple step can make the difference between a message that lands and one that's lost.

When Words Fail

There will be moments when language simply isn't working—for them or for you. That's okay. Presence doesn't require words. Sitting together quietly, holding hands, sharing a cup of tea—these are complete conversations.

Communication is not just about exchanging information. It's about making another person feel seen, heard, and safe. You can do all three without saying a word.

Our Good Moments
Pause & Reflect

Not everything about this season is loss. Write down the moments of light so you can find them again on darker days.

A recent moment when we really connected . . .

Something that still makes them light up . . .

* * *

A conversation I want to remember . . .

Something I've learned about reaching them . . .

* * *

A small, ordinary moment that mattered more than it should have . . .

Part Three
Practical Tools

Chapter 6
What to Track and Why

Tracking isn't surveillance. It isn't hovering. It's paying attention in a way that serves both of you.

When you're living inside the daily reality of caregiving, it can be hard to see patterns. Did the confusion start after the medication change, or was it already happening? Are the hard days clustering around certain times, activities, or environments? Is the sleep getting worse, or does it just feel that way because you're exhausted?

A few simple notes—even just a line or two each day—can reveal patterns that are invisible in the moment. They also give you something concrete to share with doctors, who rely on your observations far more than most people realize. You are the expert on your loved one's daily life. The tracking pages that follow are designed to make that expertise visible.

What's Worth Noting

You don't need to track everything. Focus on what helps you see patterns and communicate with the medical team:

31

- **Sleep**: How long, how restful, any disruptions or wandering.
- **Mood**: General emotional tone of the day. What seemed to help or hurt.
- **Confusion triggers**: New environments, crowds, overstimulation, fatigue.
- **Good moments**: What activities, people, or settings brought them alive.
- **Appetite and hydration**: Any noticeable changes.
- **Medication effects**: Anything new since a dosage or medication change.

Keep it simple. A few words each day is infinitely more useful than an elaborate system you abandon after a week.

NOTES:

How Was Today?
Daily Tracking

Photocopy this page or simply repeat the pattern in a notebook.

Date: ___________________

Overall Day: Hard / Mixed / Good / Great

Sleep last night:

Mood patterns today:

What helped today:

What was difficult:

Notes for the doctor:

* * *

Date: ___________________

Overall Day: Hard / Mixed / Good / Great

Sleep last night:

Mood patterns today:

What helped today:

What was difficult:

Notes for the doctor:

* * *

Date: _____________________
    Overall Day: Hard / Mixed / Good / Great
    Sleep last night:
    Mood patterns today:
    What helped today:
    What was difficult:
    Notes for the doctor:

* * *

Date: _____________________
    Overall Day: Hard / Mixed / Good / Great
    Sleep last night:
    Mood patterns today:
    What helped today:
    What was difficult:
    Notes for the doctor:

* * *

Date: _____________________
    Overall Day: Hard / Mixed / Good / Great
    Sleep last night:
    Mood patterns today:
    What helped today:
    What was difficult:
    Notes for the doctor:

Chapter 7

Navigating Medical Appointments

Doctors' appointments can be stressful for everyone involved. Your loved one may be anxious, embarrassed, or confused by the clinical environment. You may feel pressure to convey everything important in a fifteen-minute window. And the doctor, however well-intentioned, is working with limited information unless you provide it.

Preparation makes a measurable difference. Walking in with a simple one-page summary of what you've observed—changes, concerns, questions—transforms the appointment from a scramble into a conversation.

Before the Visit

Review your tracking notes from the past few weeks. What patterns stand out? What's changed? What worries you most?

Consider whether there are things you need to discuss with the doctor that might upset or confuse your loved one. Many doctors are willing to speak with caregivers privately by phone, or to receive a written note before the appointment. Don't feel guilty about this. It's not going behind their back. It's making sure the doctor has the full picture.

If possible, bring someone with you to take notes. Appointments move fast, and it's hard to listen, advocate, and absorb information all at the same time.

Questions Worth Asking

You won't always have time for a long list, but these are consistently useful:

- What changes should prompt a call to your office?
- What should we expect in the next six to twelve months?
- Are there any medications that should be reviewed?
- What support services do you recommend at this stage?
- Is it time to consider occupational therapy or speech therapy?

Doctor Visit Prep Sheet
Tear Out or Photocopy

Appointment Date: _______________________

Doctor: _______________________

Top 3 Concerns Right Now:

Changes Since Last Visit:

Questions I Need Answered:

Current Medications:

Chapter 8
Building Your Support Team

Here is a truth that most caregivers learn too late: you cannot do this alone. That's not a weakness. It's not a failure. It's math. The demands of caregiving will, over time, exceed what any single human being can sustain. Building your support system now—while you still have the energy and clarity to do it—is one of the most important things you can do.

Asking for help is not a sign that you're failing. It's a sign that you understand what's ahead.

Types of Support

Medical support: Your loved one's primary care physician, neurologist, or geriatrician. A geriatric care manager, if available, can be invaluable for coordinating care.

Practical support: People who can help with meals, errands, transportation, household tasks. This might be family, friends, neighbors, hired help, or a combination.

Emotional support: People you can be honest with about how you're actually doing. A support group—online or in person—

38

can be transformative, because you're with people who truly understand.

Respite support: Someone who can take over for a few hours, a day, a weekend, so you can rest. Adult day programs, in-home respite care, and trusted friends or family members all count.

Starting the Conversation

Many caregivers struggle to ask for help because they feel they should be able to handle it, or because they don't want to burden others. But people in your life often want to help—they just don't know how.

Be specific. "I'm fine" teaches people to stop asking. "Could you sit with Mom for two hours on Thursday so I can go to a doctor's appointment?" gives them something concrete they can say yes to. Most people respond better to a clear, specific request than a vague expression of need.

Resources to Know About

Alzheimer's Association 24/7 Helpline: 1-800-272-3900. Staffed around the clock by specialists who can provide information, referrals, and crisis support.

Eldercare Locator: 1-800-677-1116. A national service that connects you to local aging resources in your community.

Family Caregiver Alliance: caregiver.org. Information, support groups, and practical tools for family caregivers.

Your local Area Agency on Aging: Search at eldercare.acl.gov. They can connect you with local services including adult day programs, meal delivery, and respite care.

You don't have to use all of these. But know they exist. When the day comes that you need them—and it likely will—you'll be glad you didn't have to start searching from scratch.

My Support Network
Pause & Reflect

You don't have to have all of these filled in right now. But naming what you have—and what you need—is the first step.

People I can call when I need to talk . . .

My Support Network

People who can provide practical help (errands, meals, sitting with my person).

Our primary doctor and any specialists.

What I most need right now that I haven't asked for.

My Support Network

A boundary I need to set or a responsibility I need to hand off . . .

Part Four

Preserving Together

This section is different. It's not about managing symptoms or preparing for appointments. It's about gathering—while you still can—the stories, the history, the texture of a life.

Not for posterity alone, but for right now. The act of remembering together is its own kind of medicine. When your person tells you a story from their childhood, they're not just recalling information. They're inhabiting a version of themselves that feels whole and vivid and real. And you're being invited in.

Some of these prompts are meant to be completed together—you asking, them answering, both of you lingering in the telling. Others are for you alone, to capture the details you don't want to lose. There's no wrong way to use them. Write as much or as little as you need.

The stories don't have to be accurate to be true. What matters is the telling. What matters is being together in the telling.

Childhood & Family
Remembering Together

Where did you grow up? What did it look like?

What's your earliest memory?

* * *

Who was your favorite relative, and why?

What got you in trouble as a kid?

* * *

What did your mother's kitchen smell like?

Young Adulthood
Remembering Together

What was your first real job?

How did you meet the love of your life?

* * *

What did you dream of becoming?

What was the best decision you ever made?

* * *

Where did you feel most at home?

Life's Texture
Remembering Together

What song takes you right back?

What's the best meal you ever ate?

* * *

What are you proudest of?

What do you wish people knew about you?

* * *

What advice would you give your younger self?

What I Want to Remember
For the Caregiver Alone

These pages are just for you. Write what you need to hold onto.

A story I never want to forget . . .

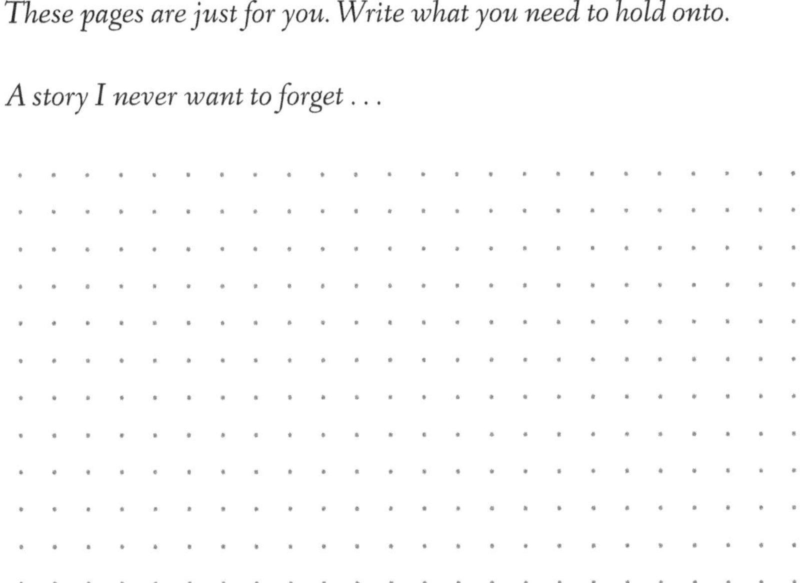

The way they laugh . . .

* * *

Something they always say . . .

How I want to remember this time . . .

* * *

What I most want them to know . . .

A Favorite Photo

Attach or tape a photo here that matters to you both.

What makes this photo matter . . .

Part Five

Taking Care of You

Chapter 9
The Weight You're Carrying

There's a kind of grief that has no funeral.

It's the grief of losing someone who's still sitting across from you at breakfast. Still breathing, still present, still—in so many ways—the person you've always known. But different. And becoming more different, slowly, in ways that only you can see.

Clinicians call this anticipatory grief. The name is clinical, but the experience is anything but. It's waking up next to someone and missing them. It's mourning the future you planned together. It's the strange guilt of grieving a person who is still alive.

Some days you'll feel tender and patient. Some days you'll feel resentful, exhausted, desperate for your old life. Both are true. Both are allowed. The guilt you feel when you wish for escape? That's not a character flaw. That's a human heart under impossible pressure.

The Loneliness of Invisible Caregiving

In the early stage, your caregiving may be largely invisible to the outside world. Your person looks fine. They sound fine. The help you're providing—the quiet monitoring, the gentle redirections, the emotional labor of holding it all together—doesn't look like caregiving to anyone who isn't doing it.

This invisibility can be profoundly isolating. You may feel like you're performing normalcy while privately falling apart. You may stop talking about it because you're tired of people minimizing what you're going through.

If that's where you are, hear this: what you're doing is real, it's hard, and it counts. You don't need anyone's permission to name it.

The Guilt That Comes with Love

Caregiver guilt is almost universal, and it's almost never warranted.

You'll feel guilty for losing your temper. For wanting time alone. For resenting the person you love. For not doing enough, or not doing it well enough, or for not being the endlessly patient saint that nobody actually is.

Let me say something clearly: you are allowed to be a whole person with needs, limits, and bad days. Caring for someone with dementia doesn't require you to erase yourself. In fact, the more you tend to your own humanity, the more you'll have to offer theirs.

Chapter 10
Sustainable Caregiving

You cannot pour from a dry vessel. You've probably heard this before. It's become a cliché in caregiving circles, which is unfortunate, because it's also completely true.

Sustainable caregiving isn't about spa days and bubble baths. It's about the unsexy, daily practice of preserving enough of yourself to keep going. It's about small acts of self-preservation that you can actually do, even on the worst days.

Small Acts That Matter

Self-care doesn't have to be grand. Sometimes it's:

- Drinking a cup of coffee while it's still hot.
- Stepping outside for five minutes of fresh air.
- Calling someone who makes you laugh.
- Going to bed fifteen minutes earlier.
- Saying no to one thing you don't have the energy for.
- Letting the house be messy.

- Eating a meal sitting down, with no one else's needs on your mind.

The standard doesn't have to be thriving. *Some days, the standard is surviving—and that's good enough.*

Warning Signs You're Running on Empty

Caregivers often don't notice their own decline until it becomes a crisis. Check in with yourself honestly. If several of these ring true, it's time to ask for more help:

- Sleeping too little or too much
- Snapping at small things
- Neglecting your own medical appointments
- Withdrawing from friends and activities you used to enjoy
- Feeling numb, hopeless, or trapped
- Using food, alcohol, or other substances to cope
- Dreading each day before it begins
- Physical symptoms: headaches, back pain, constant fatigue

Recognizing these signs isn't weakness. It's wisdom. And asking for help before you hit bottom is one of the bravest things a caregiver can do.

Setting Boundaries Without Guilt

Boundaries aren't selfish. They're the infrastructure that makes long-term caregiving possible.

A boundary might be: I won't answer the phone after 9 p.m. unless it's an emergency. Or: I need one afternoon a week that's mine. Or: I'm not going to argue about things that don't matter.

The people who push back on your boundaries are usually not the ones doing the caregiving. You don't owe anyone an explanation for protecting your capacity to keep showing up.

Taking Your Own Pulse
Pause & Reflect

Be honest. Nobody is grading this.

Right now, I feel . . .

What I've been neglecting in myself . . .

* * *

One small thing that refills me . . .

What I need permission to let go of . . .

* * *

Something I'm doing well, even if it doesn't feel like enough . . .

Notes & Questions
For Later

A place for concerns to jot down, questions that come to you at 2 a.m., things you want to bring up at the next appointment, or anything else that needs a home.

Notes & Questions

A Final Word

This season will ask more of you than seems possible.

There will be days that break you open. Days when the weight of what's happening feels unbearable, when you can't imagine doing this for one more hour, let alone one more year.

There will also be moments of startling grace. A shared laugh that catches you off guard. A sudden clarity in their eyes that takes your breath away. A hand reaching for yours in the dark. Moments when you realize that love doesn't require memory to be real.

You won't do this perfectly. No one does. You'll lose your patience. You'll say the wrong thing. You'll wonder, on the hard days, whether you're doing any of it right.

You are.

You're here, showing up, holding on while slowly learning to let go. You're doing the tender, relentless, unglamorous work of loving someone through a passage that frightens you both. And you're doing it not because it's easy, but because they matter. Because you matter. Because this strange, heartbreaking, beautiful season matters.

That's not nothing. That's everything.

About the Author

L J Ribar is a writer and former software engineer who spent forty-five years building systems before turning to the work of building stories. He writes about the ordinary extraordinary — the quiet seasons of life that change everything without making a sound.

The In-Between series grew from his belief that the hardest moments in caregiving aren't medical. They're human. And that the people navigating those moments deserve a companion that speaks to them honestly, without platitudes, and with the respect they've earned.

L J lives and writes from an RV with his wife, the novelist Joy Ann Ribar, traveling across America and collecting the stories that make up the places between here and there.

Connect with L J at LJRibar.com and WineGlassPress.com.

Also by
L J Ribar

Sharing a Long Goodbye

A husband's story of cancer, loss, and learning to live again

Second, Expanded Edition

When my wife Lesa was diagnosed with advanced cancer, I thought my job was simple: be strong, take notes, drive to appointments, hold things together for everyone else.

What I didn't understand was that I was beginning my own kind of long goodbye.

If you're reading a book about early dementia, you may know something about that already. A long goodbye isn't a single moment. It's a season—sometimes years long—where you love someone while slowly losing pieces of them, and of the life you built together. The details differ with cancer and dementia, but some of the questions are very much the same: How do I stay present when I can't fix what's happening? What do I do with the anger, fear, and guilt that come in waves? Who takes care of me while I'm taking care of them?

It's not a medical textbook. It's the everyday reality of trying to be a decent husband while the person you love most is suffering.

Sharing a Long Goodbye tells the story of our five-year journey—diagnosis, hospital corridors, chemo cycles, the long stretches of waiting, and finally home hospice in our dining room. It looks closely at what it's like to live through serious illness and death up close: what you might see in the last weeks, how hospice teams can actually help, how faith can feel both fragile and strangely solid in the same season, and what "showing up" looks like when you feel completely helpless.

The second edition of this book also includes the practical things I wished someone had handed me on an index card in a waiting room: questions to ask the doctor when your mind goes blank, what to pack for long days at the hospital, a letter to the woman who is worried about her husband, and a gentle guide for friends and church folks who want to help but don't know how.

You don't have to read it straight through. Many people dip into the sections that match where they are: early diagnosis, the heavy middle, hospice and the end, or the strange life that begins after. My hope is that it feels less like an instruction manual and more like another husband sitting beside you saying, "I've been there. You're not alone."

Though Lesa's illness was cancer, not dementia, the heart of the book is about caregiving, grief that starts long before death, and the slow, uneven work of learning to live again. If you've found echoes of your own story in these pages, you may find a companion in Sharing a Long Goodbye as well.

— L J Ribar

Key Resources
Quick Reference

Alzheimer's Association 24/7 Helpline
1-800-272-3900 | alz.org

Eldercare Locator
1-800-677-1116 | eldercare.acl.gov

Family Caregiver Alliance
1-800-445-8106 | caregiver.org

National Alliance for Caregiving
caregiving.org

AARP Caregiver Resource Center
aarp.org/caregiving

Our Information

Primary Doctor: _______________________________________

Neurologist/Specialist:

____

Pharmacy: _______________________________________

Local Support Group:

____

Emergency Contact:

____

Home Health/Respite:

____

Insurance Info: _______________________________________